Manage your career

**How to develop your career
in the right direction**

A & C Black • London

First published in 2006 by
A & C Black Publishers Ltd
38 Soho Square
London W1D 3HB

British Library Cataloguing in Publication Data
A CIP record for this book is available from the British Library.

ISBN-10: 0–7136–7522–5
ISBN-13: 978–0–7136–7522–1

Design by Fiona Pike, Pike Design, Winchester
Typeset by RefineCatch Limited, Bungay, Suffolk
Printed in Italy by Legoprint

A & C Black uses paper produced with elemental chlorine free pulp,
harvested from managed sustainable forests.

Contents

Is your career on the right tracks?

Answer the questions and work out your score, then read the guidance points for advice on taking your career in the right direction.

Does your job utilise your main strengths?
a) I don't know what my strengths are.
b) Not really.
c) Yes.

Are you happy with where you see yourself in 3 years' time?
a) No. I'd like to have had a more varied career by then.
b) Fairly.
c) I am concerned that I won't have had enough of a life outside work.

What is your next goal?
a) To have a career within my area of interest.
b) Nothing realistic.
c) To sort out some personal issues.

Have you considered a career change recently?
a) Yes.
b) I would like to but I am worried about lack of security.
c) No.

If the opportunity arose to change jobs, how easy would it be for you to accept?
a) I doubt it would arise.
b) I would be concerned about the risks.
c) Very.

Do you experience stress at work?
a) No.
b) I suppose so—sometimes I can't sleep.
c) Yes.

Does your current CV accurately reflect you as a person and as an employee?
a) Not really—it's functional, not personal.
b) I haven't updated it for ages.
c) Not as a person. I seem to have no life outside of work.

Is there any chance that you might be promoted in your current workplace?
a) No.
b) There are opportunities, but I doubt they will come my way.
c) Yes, if I continue to work hard.

I make decisions:
a) Only when I have to.
b) Very rarely!
c) Often and quickly.

When faced with different types of risk (emotional or financial, for example), I am generally:

a) Nervous.
b) Cautious.
c) Impulsive.

a = 1, b = 2, and c = 3.

Now add up your scores.

8–14: You really should consider moving on from your current situation. To avoid another unrewarding job, be sure of what it is that you want from a career (chapter 2 will help you). Make sure you have done plenty of research before you make the move (see chapter 3).

15–19: Though you seem to be managing your career, make sure you are not sticking at something just because it is a safe option. In 20 years' time will you be able to look back on your life and say that you achieved what you wanted? Chapter 1 will help you to decide whether your existing job is really right for you. If it is not, chapters 3 and 4 will help you to decide whether to move on and how to achieve greater job satisfaction.

20–24: You seem to be focussed on making the most of your talents—but be careful that being a success at work does not override your ability to enjoy the rest of your life and still achieve those personal ambitions which you have perhaps neglected. Chapter 5 will help you to identify whether you have a problem with stress, and can help you to put your priorities back in order.

Making sure you're in the right job

The last time many of us thought seriously about our careers was at school or university. We set out on our career paths with a clear starting point and some idea of what we might move on to, but a complete blank for what was to come after that. If you find yourself at a bit of a crossroads, then it's time to take action and to actively manage your career to make sure you're getting the most from it, both financially and in terms of your personal development.

It's rare these days that employers provide us with career-long job security, so it's up to us to craft our own career strategies and manage them carefully. The alternative? Ending up on the sidelines while opportunities pass us by. This chapter offers help on the first step towards managing your career: assessing your present situation, and deciding whether you are really heading for where you want to be.

Step one: Stop and think

It's human nature to wonder, regardless of what we happen to be doing, whether we ought in fact to be doing something else. This is particularly the case with jobs; most people spend at least some of their working life questioning themselves and their careers and speculating about whether there are other occupations 'out there' which might make better use of their time and efforts.

When you feel you have reached an impasse, or when outside factors force you to stop and think, it is important to ask yourself:

- Would I be happy to continue what I have been doing for the rest of my working life?
- What do I really want to do?
- How will I make the transition?

As with most things, it helps to analyse the situation objectively. A job is made up of many elements—it's not just the actual day-to-day work—and it's the combination of these elements that makes it suitable or otherwise. Your *skills*, of course, are fundamental to what you do, but are these the same as your *strengths*? And what about your values? Then there's the company you work for: is it the right size, in the right industry sector, with the right culture? Then there are the questions about who you work with, what your boss is like, whether you have suitable levels of responsibility, what kind of pay and benefits you receive, and so on and so forth.

By looking at all these factors, you can work out whether your job is suitable for you, and, if not, what needs to be put right.

Step two: Identify your areas of interest

First and foremost, if you're not interested in what you're doing, you're never going to be able to put your heart into your work. So, if your company, industry, subject, or sector doesn't engage you, it might be a good idea to go back to basics and identify one that does.

Is there a **topic, issue, or activity** that you've enjoyed or had in your mind for a long time—art, maths, helping others, science, construction, the environment, for example?

Or does a **specific job** attract you—possibly something that you've dismissed in the past for some reason, or one based on something that you do as a hobby? Maybe you'd like to be a website designer, financial advisor, music teacher, painter/decorator, or landscape gardener, for instance?

Or perhaps there's a **specific industry** that fascinates you—advertising, manufacturing, health care, electronics, entertainment, whatever—that you could explore further. Any area that piques your curiosity or makes you want to know more is a good place to start!

Step three: Pinpoint your strengths

Once you've settled on an area of interest, the most important aspect of any job is whether it makes the best use of your individual strengths. If it does, many of the other elements of satisfactory employment—self-fulfilment, motivation, a sense of achievement, and so on—fall naturally into place. So the first thing to do is to assess what your strengths are and whether or not you're using these in your current position. Your strengths can be defined as the areas where your interests and your abilities overlap; in other words, the business activities that you both like *and* are good at. The two aren't necessarily the same!

Take a look at the table opposite and, being as honest as you can, put ticks against the activities you are interested in, and then against the ones you're good at. The rows where you get ticks in both 'Interest' and 'Ability' are your main strengths. You may find there are some surprises in your results! The list of activities is by no means exhaustive, so add in any others that apply particularly to you.

Once you've identified your strengths, consider whether and how you're using them in your job:

✔ Could you be doing more with them?

✔ Are there other areas of the organisation which might benefit from them?

Interest	Activities	Ability
	Research	
	Analysis	
	Interpretation	
	Problem-solving	
	Budgeting	
	Planning	
	Process Management	
	Leadership	
	Decision-making	
	Follow through	
	Administration	
	Mentoring	
	Innovation	
	Imagination	
	Vision	
	Project management	
	Empathy	
	Listening	
	Written presentation	
	Verbal presentation	
	Negotiation	
	Initiative	
	Flexibility	
	Team working	
	Facilitating	
	Installing	
	Operating	

✔ Could you take on different responsibilities, or would a shift in the focus of your job suit you better?

If you feel that you have more to offer, try talking to your boss—any sensible employer will understand the benefits of making the most of their employees' strengths, and will value people who are proactive in the way they approach their work.

TOP TIP
Unless you know deep-down that you are going to move on, make sure you use positive language when you broach this issue with your boss, and be as upbeat as you can so that you don't panic him or her into thinking that you are going to leave immediately.

Being good at what you do doesn't necessarily mean that you are in the right job. There's more to doing a job than simply being able to fulfil the requirements. You could be a very good builder because you're physically strong and fit, but you may have the soul of a philosopher or a secret yearning to be a garden designer. It's when your interests and abilities coincide that you find yourself in the ideal job. That said, however, if you are happy in your work and don't feel the need to stretch yourself in other directions, you probably are in the right job—at least for the time being.

As every person has many facets to his or her personality, most people could do any of a number of different jobs and be equally happy and satisfied. Broadly speaking, however, there are four main considerations which need to be fulfilled in a work context for someone to be content with his or her job. These are:

- areas of interest
- job strengths
- behaviour under normal and stress conditions
- social perceptions and compatibility with others.

If you find that you have a mismatch between any of these four and the job you are doing, it is unlikely that you will be comfortable in that job.

Step four: Consider the organisation you work for

A good match between your strengths and the work you are doing proves that you are in the right *type* of job. But is it in the right place? For example, you could be an accountant in a big blue-chip corporation, when really you'd be happiest running the finances for a small family-run firm.

Think about the organisation you work for. How big is it? Would you prefer to work with more or fewer people? Apart from size, here's a list of other factors you might consider:

- Public/private sector
- Profit/non-profit

- National/multinational
- Academic
- Product/service
- Centralised/decentralised
- Financial condition
- Political climate
- Company growth, current and future
- Stability
- Reputation
- Market dependency
- Profitability
- Vulnerability to takeover

Step five: Think about your rewards

Now think about the rewards you receive for the work you do. While these shouldn't necessarily be the most important factor of a job, obviously you need to have your needs met. This is even more the case if your circumstances mean that you require a certain level of income or security—if you have children, for example, or a mortgage.

Remember that it's not just salary that should be considered—other benefits are equally important. A pension, life and disability insurance, health benefits, or a severance package could be vital if you have a family; a bonus scheme or other performance incentive might be a prime motivator if you're the kind of person who likes to have targets. If you're expected to travel or relocate, what provision is made for moving expenses, temporary living costs, or housing subsidy? Does the holiday entitlement give you enough time with the children? What about flexible working or study leave?

Step six: Evaluate yourself

Then there's your own personality to consider. It is extremely stressful to have to try to fill a role that simply isn't 'you'. Much of this comes down to your own personal values, but useful areas to examine are as follows:

- **Interpersonal**. Do you like working with other people? Is it essential to you that colleagues are also friends?
- **Responsibility**. How much do you like? Do you prefer to manage, or would you rather be managed?
- **Pressure**. A high-stress hospital ward could be dreadful for a postman; a peaceful publishing office might bore a sales rep to death. How much can you cope with?
- **Potential**. Are you a high flier with ambitions for regular promotion, or do you want a steady job that will support your family?
- **Compatibility with lifestyle**. Do you have hobbies or non-work commitments that you don't want to compromise, or would you love lots of business travel and high-powered meetings?

Common mistakes

✗ You bail out too early

Nothing in life is ever perfect, and it's tempting during a rough patch simply to blame your troubles on your job and go hunting for another one. However, financial considerations aside, it's always worth pausing to consider before you do this. What else may be making you feel dissatisfied? Is it someone or something that could be sorted out with a little patience and effort? Could it be that you're simply bored at the moment? If you *do* decide it's time to move on, make sure you've done your homework first (there's more on this in chapter 6) so that your new role brings real benefits and you don't simply move from one unsatisfactory situation into another.

✗ You forget the importance of your own attitude

There is an old song that contains the line, 'If you can't be with the one you love, love the one you're with'. This is very useful to bear in mind in the context of your job. If it's not easy for you to leave your current working situation, your challenge is to discover its benefits rather than fretting about being stuck. Quite often, contentment comes from the way you choose to perceive things. It might be an old fashioned thing to say, but counting your blessings—rather than cursing your luck—can make all the difference to how you feel about something!

STEPS TO SUCCESS

✔ Understand that job satisfaction results from many different elements: having an interest in your work, utilising your strengths, etc.

✔ Your skills are not the same as your strengths. Identify what you are interested in and what you do best, and look for areas where these come together.

✔ Talk to your employers—if they're not making the most of your strengths it's best all round if they address this.

✔ There is more to a job than just being good at it or earning a suitable wage; assess whether your working life is compatible with your personality and values.

✔ Keep in mind the context of your job. Rather than worry about being trapped, work out the benefits of your current situation and make the most of them.

Useful links

HR-Guide.Com:
www.hr-guide.com
HRM Guide:
www.hrmguide.co.uk
hrVillage.com:
www.hrvillage.com

Creating a career plan

When jobs were for life, you decided what line of work you wanted, worked hard, and the career path was pretty much mapped out for you. The working world has changed. Now individuals wanting to maximise their potential will take a much more active part in shaping their career. Career planning today needs to be a frequent, dynamic process of self-awareness, market and trend analysis, planning, development, and self-marketing—all of which will help you to manage your career in the best way for you.

The good news is that career paths are more flexible. Individuals can choose a spiral one, stepping through different fields or functions. Many enlightened employers encourage cross-fertilisation of ideas through diversity in their workforce and value the different perspectives offered by those from outside their industry.

As career breaks are more common today, even transitory career paths are possible. These are popular with people who like variety, novelty, or have other worthwhile priorities. If you require periods of employment interspersed with breaks, be it for study, travel, raising a family, starting a business, or caring for elderly or unwell family members, this option could be for you.

There are, however, still expert career paths for those who want to specialise in a particular field and linear careers for those who enjoy the challenge, responsibility, and status of climbing the hierarchical ladder. Whatever your set of circumstances, think about this: what does your career need to do for *you*?

Step one: Be self-aware

Review your career so far, asking yourself some key questions:

✔ What expertise do you have?

✔ What achievements are you proud of?

✔ What work have you received praise and recognition for?

✔ What were the outcomes of these achievements for your clients, team, or organisation?

✔ What flair or talents have you not yet fully used?

✔ Do you have areas of untapped potential?

Also consider the skills you've used throughout your career

so far and any differences in the way you've worked. For each job you've held,

✔ Go through a typical working week and, on a separate piece of paper or Post-it® note, write down each skill, strength, or knowledge area that you have used.

✔ Cluster your notes, grouping those that fit together and giving each group a title, such as 'Organising', 'Communicating', or 'People skills'.

Doing this will identify and organise your transferable skills and help you to be clearer about what you're offering other employers.

✔ Finally, draw other elements into the mix. What does your career need to do for you (and your family)? What do you value in work? What makes a job satisfying? What would you/do you hate in a job?

Thinking about these questions will help you to identify your needs and constraints, such as financial obligations or geographical preferences.

Step two: Do a market and trend analysis

Next you need to focus on the market you're working in and which way that seems to be moving. What do you like about the market you're currently in? What are the trends within this function and industry? How might these affect your prospects? Think in broad terms about who might have a need for your skills. What goals or problems could you help them with and what else can you offer them?

These are big and wide-ranging questions, so, to help you focus on them, do some research. Use the Internet and your network of friends and colleagues to expand your knowledge of companies and organisations and of their internal trends and needs. Read all you can in journals and newspapers about the markets you are most interested in and identify relevant professional bodies for information on trends and the market for relevant skills. Libraries and Chambers of Commerce can be good sources of local information. The more questions you ask, the more you will know what other information you need, and research often gets easier as you go along.

TOP TIP
If you are naturally curious and chatty, you could start your research by talking to people. Make use of your contacts and ask for names and contact details of people who might be able to help with each of the options you're considering. This approach not only increases your network, but it also gets you the targeted information you need. It may also put you in touch with contacts who can open doors for you.

**On the other hand, you may prefer to start
with some Internet or library research and
save the networking until you feel better
informed. Neither approach is right or wrong,
but people who use *both* approaches are
likely to be the best prepared, most
knowledgeable, and 'luckiest' when it comes
to opportunities.**

Step three: Plan ahead

Be clear about how you want your research and planning to
fit together. Ask yourself what you'd like your life to be like in
three years' time and write down what comes to mind in as
much detail as you can. Write in the present tense, as if it has
already happened. Then repeat this for one year's time, six
months' time and one month's time.

This '3-1-6-1' plan gives clarity and motivation for the long-
term future. It breaks down the bigger picture of your life into
an actionable plan that you can start on right now.

A **reality check** will help you recognise the right
opportunity when it arises. Spend time on this when you are
job-hunting. Divide a page into four quarters, headed
'Organisation', 'Role', 'Boss', and 'Package'. Now ask
yourself what you want from your next career move. Think
about the 'ingredients' that would make up your ideal role,
putting these into the appropriate sections on your page.
Once your criteria are mapped out in this way, you'll have a

visual aid that will help you to weigh up the opportunities that come your way. When you're invited to interview for a new job, you can use the sheet to come up with strong, targeted questions about the potential role and the organisation. See chapter 8 for a more detailed explanation.

TOP TIP

Know the difference between a career plan and a development plan. Your career plan maps out long-term and more immediate objectives and how you want your life and work to fit together. Your development plan maps out the skills and experience gaps for the different steps along the way and how you will address them. In effect, the development plan enables the career plan to work.

Step four: Develop yourself

You have now identified your own skills and both your short- and long-term goals. Is there a direct match already or will employers see gaps? If there are, specify what those gaps are and prioritise them, working out what you need to learn. Divide each gap into bite-sized chunks of learning or experience required.

How do you learn best? Do you prefer to read books, listen to an expert, try things out yourself, or practise with supervision? Knowing your preferred learning style is important to your planning.

Finally, you have to be sure that you're motivated to do this learning. If you are, go back to your '3-1-6-1' plan and write in what it will be like to have filled these gaps at the relevant stages. If, on the other hand, you have more to do than you think you'll likely be motivated to do, your plan is unrealistic and needs to be changed. Don't think, though, that all changes need to be drastic—sometimes a modified timescale is the only tweak needed to allow your dream to happen.

Step five: Market yourself

Identify the stage you are at and your objectives. Let's look at three examples.

During the honeymoon period in a **new job**, your objective is to establish good communication channels with your new colleagues and contacts and build a practical network. Here, then, marketing yourself will focus on attracting the interest of people who will make your work easier.

Once you feel **established** in your new role, your objective is to make sure that interesting work is offered to you, so self-marketing in *this* context will focus more on bringing your successes and achievements to light.

When **looking for new roles**, your objective is to attract offers that meet your criteria. Your self-marketing will now focus on getting yourself noticed by the right employers.

As we can see, self-marketing will change in nature depending on where you are in your career and what your ideal next step is. Whatever you're doing, however, keep in mind your 'audience' and what is important to them. You may be offering to solve problems, deliver a product or service, improve quality or develop something new. To grab and maintain their attention, you need to focus on the relevant outcomes of your activities: improvements in efficiency, customer satisfaction and retention, or increased profits.

TOP TIP

If you are worried about whether frequent job moves will look bad on your CV, consider what is 'normal' for your market. In IT, for example, regular moves are common. A CV that shows frequent moves is less likely to be frowned on if the skills offered and achievements shown are relevant to the job you're applying for now. If it is clear that in each role you've occupied you've been promoted or selected for specific strengths or skills, then employers will see you as a sought-after individual rather than a job hopper.

Common mistakes

✗ You forget to market yourself

Don't assume that your work alone will get you noticed. Self-marketing is what makes the difference between a good job well done and a good job resulting in a promotion. If you are looking for a move up the ladder, keep up the momentum and don't wait to market yourself until you need your next role urgently—try to get into the habit of doing it and of raising your profile gradually but consistently.

✗ You have unrealistic ambitions

If you don't take the time to identify trends and their impact on your market, you'll end up with a career plan that's completely unrealistic. The wealth of information on the Internet in particular means that there's little excuse for remaining ignorant about issues that may affect your future success. Even if you're not online at home, you can use an Internet café or visit your local library to find out what you need to know. Make it your business to be informed and don't be afraid to ask 'difficult' questions of people in the know—experts love the opportunity to shine and will be flattered that you've asked them.

✗ You're not flexible

A plan is there to make your objectives happen, and so is tied in to real life. Just as life shifts and changes all the time, so must you and your objectives. Take time to review your plans regularly so that you can take into account unexpected twists and turns at work or other areas of your life. The beauty of a '3-1-6-1' plan is that it forces you to do this—each month you have to decide what to put into this month's plan so that, in turn, you can make the next 6 months' plan happen. Re-examine your chosen strategy as often as you need to make sure it still describes the future you want.

✗ You don't do anything

A plan works by provoking specific and related actions which together create the desired effect. There's absolutely no point in writing a plan and then leaving it to gather dust. You have to be ready to keep plugging away at your To-do list in order to get a good result. You may get downhearted at times—you're only human—but try to keep setbacks in perspective and to keep your goal in sight.

STEPS TO SUCCESS

✔ Know what you can offer an employer as well as what you expect an employer to offer you. Review your career history to identify both needs and constraints.

✔ Do your homework! Through the Internet, libraries, and personal contacts, you can identify market trends that might affect your prospects.

✔ Have long- and short-term goals. Assess what new skills you need to develop in order to achieve these goals and give yourself a realistic time scale.

✔ Remember that you must be proactive—recognition and development will not automatically come to you.

✔ Market yourself depending on which stage of your career you are at and where you are hoping to go.

✔ Be optimistic and keep pushing—if you are well-informed and constantly active, opportunities are more likely to present themselves.

Useful links

BBC Radio 1:
www.bbc.co.uk/radio1/onelife/work/index.shtml
British Chambers of Commerce:
www.chamberonline.co.uk
The Open University's Careers Advisory Service:
www.open.ac.uk/career/index.php
Totaljobs.com:
www.totaljobs.com

Making the decision to take a risky career move

Everything in business today is risky. There is no such thing as a safe bet. It's certainly risky to leave a familiar job with routines, expectations, and objectives that you're comfortable with to test the limits of your courage and skills in a strange environment. But, as thousands of redundant employees in global companies can attest, it's not exactly safe holding onto a job that's as dependable as a leaky lifeboat. Whether you should decide to make that risky career move is entirely up to the nature of the risk and your ability to cope with the possible negative consequences.

The risk itself may be made up of any number of factors, such as your ability to move into an unfamiliar job or your ability to move into an unfamiliar organisation. Are you jumping from an Old Economy position to a New Economy one? Or are you leaping back into the Old Economy world after trying your luck in a high-tech, high-pressure, go-go New Economy environment? Are you considering leaving a stable, secure position that's limited in its prospects in favour of the white-knuckle environment of a bootstrap start-up? Are you

about to move from a solid public organisation into a family-owned business? Is the family that owns the business your own?

Step one: Identify what 'acceptable risk' means to you

Only you know the risks you're ready to take in terms of your career. If you're young and single, with no obligations other than to yourself, you can probably afford to take on a few risky moves. These high-profile actions can give you early boosts that could position you for more momentum-driven rewards later in your career. If you're older, perhaps with a family or other responsibilities, you may not be quite as willing to try your luck with a high-risk/high-reward venture, such as a start-up enterprise.

TOP TIP

If you feel uncomfortable in risky situations but still want to grow in your career, remember that there are no guarantees in today's marketplace, so taking steps to avoid taking a risk might actually be the worst thing you could do.

For some people, the notion of going into a shaky entrepreneurial environment after drawing a steady salary for years would be intolerable. For others, depending on only one income source, as opposed to the multiple sources of revenue available to an entrepreneur, may make them feel vulnerable.

The following points are key questions to ask yourself while considering whether you should take the risk or not:

- Do the benefits outweigh the potential costs of the risk?
- How many people depend utterly on the regular income my current job provides?
- Is there a realistic back-up plan in case my gamble fails?
- Is it possible to return to my original position should I decide that my experiment was not as rewarding as I hoped?

Step two: Know your goals

Make a list of your short- and long-term objectives. Read through them and ask yourself whether your current position will help you achieve them. If your position is unlikely to help you to achieve these goals, can you make slight adjustments to your present job in order to position yourself better for achieving your dreams? Or is it necessary to leave your position entirely?

TOP TIP
Take your time! In order to ensure that you
don't regret your ultimate decision, give
yourself all the time you need to make your
choice wisely and calmly. Think it through
methodically, and then make the decision.
Whatever the outcome, be sure to learn
from the decision-making process in
some way.

Step three: Know what you value

List your less tangible values. Which of the options open to
you is most likely to help you to express those values?
Your current job or a new opportunity? Does one opportunity
actually position you to behave in ways that are contrary to
those values?

Here is one way of getting at your values: close your eyes
and imagine yourself at a much older age, looking back at
your life. First, imagine that you've had a really full and
satisfying life. Take a sheet of paper and write down the
things that you're proud to have done. What were the best
bits, that give you joy to remember? Now imagine that you're
looking back over a wasted life. What do you regret and
what do you wish you had done more of?

For example:

■ **Time and energy well spent in a full and satisfying life:**

Family: time spent talking, helping kids develop, enjoying being together, loving and being loved.

Building solid friendships for love, sharing, support, and learning.

Business: creating something bigger than myself, developing good understanding of clients' needs, developing new ways to help.

Helping others.

Developing myself to understand others better.

■ **In a wasted life I would regret:**

Not travelling and learning about other cultures.

Wasting time on appearances rather than substance.

Losing contacts with family and friends.

Staying employed all my life for the 'security'.

Wasting my creativity.

Harming others or failing to help where help was needed and I was able.

Poor health as a result of not looking after my body.

Your answers will help you to gain an idea of what you want out of life and to highlight what is missing at the moment.

Step four: Conduct a risk/benefit analysis

This is the process that will help you determine whether the potential reward outweighs the potential pain. There are several methods for analysing the potential costs, but the easiest is simply to create two columns. List the potential pain in one column and the potential reward in the other. The column that has the longer list is the one that should receive serious consideration.

A variation of this method is to assign points (from 1 to 10, for example) or potential pound values to each item. You can then either compare the grand totals or assess each pain/ reward item on its own merit.

Step five: Consider the people you'd be working with

Who do you have the most in common with? This isn't a question of who you'd be most comfortable spending an afternoon watching television or playing tennis with. Rather, whose visions and ideals are most compatible with your own? The opportunity to work with those who inspire, support, and encourage you is an exciting one, and may be something not to be missed.

Common mistakes

✗ You make the wrong choice

As there are no guarantees, there is always a chance that you'll make the wrong choice—or at least the choice that feels wrong to you as you begin to experience 'buyer's remorse'. Have faith in your risk-assessment strategy and carefully watch how that risk plays itself out. There is always something positive to be gained from every adventure.

✗ You don't make any choice at all

Contradictory as it may sound, making no choice is still making a choice. And this is the one that is almost guaranteed to net you no gain at all. Modern business is full of risky moves. Those who relish the thrill of risk, shift, and change will be the ones who will ultimately benefit from the growth and added self-awareness that comes from the adventure of being engaged in contemporary commerce.

STEPS TO SUCCESS

✔ Take time over your decision-making—it needs careful planning and thoughtful consideration of your options.

✔ 'Acceptable risk' varies from person to person. Identify how far you are able or willing to go.

✔ Decide on certain goals and assess whether or not your current position can help you achieve these.

✔ Determine what is necessary in a job in order to bring fulfilment to your life.

✔ Remember that any risk can result in a loss—so never risk more than you are willing/able to lose. There are no guarantees, but, on a positive note, benefits can be gained from most experiences.

Useful links

ALIS Career Tips:
www.alis.gov.ab.ca/tips/archive.asp?EK=130
Executive Action International:
www.executive-action.co.uk
'How to Bounce Back From Setbacks', Fast Company:
www.fastcompany.com/online/45/bounceback.html
Monster:
www.monster.co.uk

Tackling job burnout

Many people don't think much about their career until they hit a trough. This can come in many guises, and job burnout is, increasingly, one of them. Job burnout doesn't occur overnight but when it does happen, it can create a growing dread of work. In fact, it can become so strong that you can think of little else. The exact combination of symptoms varies from person to person, but here are the most common ones:

- snappiness and irritation over minor things. You may have an increasingly explosive temper with a short fuse and you may lose your sense of humour completely.
- overwhelming feelings of helplessness, frustration, and futility.
- strong and persistent negative emotions such as anger, depression, guilt, and fear. You may feel unable to pull yourself out of the cycle of negative emotions.
- difficulty in relating to others. You may feel increasingly hostile and react angrily towards others, with emotional outbursts that can damage relationships.
- withdrawal from the company of others. This is a dangerous symptom as strong social

supports act as a buffer against the effects of stress.

■ effects on your health, including 'minor' effects such as colds, headaches, insomnia, cold sores, backache, and high blood pressure. You may have a general feeling of being tired and run-down. Heart, breathing, and stomach problems are the more serious symptoms of stress.

■ problems with chemical 'solutions', ranging from coffee, cigarettes, alcohol, and sleeping pills to more addictive and dangerous substances. These can mask the root of the problem.

■ a decline in the efficiency and quality of your work. This can often lead to increased conflict and withdrawal problems, as colleagues and managers attempt to help you reverse the trend.

If you recognise any (or several) of these symptoms, your first step is to be honest with yourself and make a decision to change. Don't be afraid to ask for help. Bear in mind the sage advice of the poet, John Ruskin:

"In order that people may be happy in their work, these three things are needed: they must be fit for it; they must not do too much of it; and they must have a sense of success in it."

Step one: Admit you have a problem

Burnout is an extreme reaction to work stress. Exposure to stress produces hormonal reactions in your body. These can be divided into three stages of response, which are not specific to particular stress types and can build over time.

- **Shock and counter-shock phase:** your body reacts to perceived stress with various hormonal changes that increase your respiration and heart rate. 'Shock' can be a sudden reaction, but when you are concentrating on the task in hand, you may not notice it. If stress continues, your body increases hormone production to cope and the downwards spiral continues.
- **Resistance phase:** your body resists by releasing other hormones that dampen the effects of the shock. This adaptation allows you to cope with prolonged stress.
- **Exhaustion:** if stress is continuous, your hormone reserves drop, increasing your risk of serious illness.

Burnout can be caused by a lack of balance between important work factors:

- **Demands:** people or tasks requiring your attention and a response
- **Constraints:** lack of available resources or barriers to accessing support
- **Supports:** available resources to help you and your team

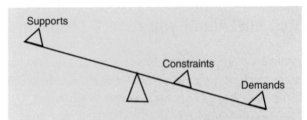

The demands and constraints of your work increase stress and the likelihood of burnout, but your supports help you to cope and reduce stress. Each of these factors can be technical, intellectual, social, financial, or psychological. The most stressful jobs are the ones where demands are high and there is little support and many constraints. The least stressful are not necessarily undemanding, but ones in which the three factors balance each other out.

You may wonder why you are suffering from burnout while your colleagues aren't. There are many reasons why stress may affect you more than your colleagues. The way you think or feel about things is important in determining whether stress produces a shock reaction or not. This is known as the person—environment fit. If you believe that you can cope with a particular stressor, you will be less affected by it.

Control protects against stress very effectively. Feeling trapped will make your job more stressful and, over time, you are more likely to suffer burnout than if you were in a similar role where you have choice and the opportunity to act at your discretion.

Your personality also controls the extent to which you are affected by job burnout. People who are habitually hostile and angry (known as type A personalities) react in a different way to stress from others. They are at greater risk of developing high blood pressure as a reaction to stress and are particularly coronary-prone if action is not taken.

Finally, events from all parts of your life can add to the stress that you are under, and even positive events, such as births and promotions, are major stressors. A poor balance between demands, supports, and constraints mixed together with major life events can be difficult to cope with.

Don't worry, though—you can bounce back. Make some immediate changes and create an ongoing stress management plan to make yourself effective in the workplace again and happier in other areas of your life. Work out clearly what stresses you, how it affects you, and what you can do about it.

Step two: Recover your health

The first port of call is your GP's. Once you've discussed your symptoms, he or she will be able to suggest a number of ways forward. For example, you may be referred to a stress counsellor, who will help you to talk about your problems in more depth and find ways to help you cope with your particular set of circumstances.

On the other hand, you may decide you'd benefit from a different tack and that you need a complete break from the demands of your job. If this is the case, you'll need to get a sick note, and, if you feel that you've been treated unfairly (that you've been placed under too much pressure by your manager, for example), the wording of this can prove to be particularly important. Organisations are becoming more aware of stress links to health and are more prepared to help you if you are open about a stress-related diagnosis.

When you feel ready to face work again, meet with your manager to discuss your future work regime, and prepare well beforehand by coming up with some specific suggestions, such as exploring the option of working from home one day a week.

TOP TIP
Relax! This is easier said than done, but the key is to understand that you need to *work* at relaxing. This may mean planning a holiday or finding a hobby or club that suits you best and then *absorbing* yourself in it. Time away from the causes of stress can help to put the situation in perspective and lead to a new approach.

Step three: Identify the sources of stress

Stress is any factor to which you have to adapt by changing your hormone levels. To help you to tackle the sources of stress in your life, follow this three-stage process:

1 Identify the **demands** that are placed upon you now, not forgetting the positive sources of stress mentioned earlier.

2 Identify the **supports** that you currently use to help you.

3 Identify the **constraints** that hinder you from meeting expectations.

TOP TIP

To help you to avoid/prepare for particularly stressful situations, it can be useful to think about previous times that were stressful for you and remember how you felt, how you reacted and behaved, what the result was, and whether, with the benefit of hindsight, you handled it in the best way possible.

Step four: Remove the sources of stress and pressure

In essence, combating job burnout effectively involves decreasing demands, increasing supports, and minimising constraints in your life, and tailoring your approach to suit you best (and not everyone else). For example, you could consider:

✔ improving the physical work environment or redesigning your job to allow greater delegation and control. This may involve some structural reorganisation or team training, so investigate this option with your manager.

✔ improving role clarity and finally resolving conflicts that crop up time and again. Both of these can make a big difference. Again, this will involve more or closer communication with your boss than you're used to. You'll both need time to adjust to this more interactive style of setting objectives, but better communication and understanding are well worth fostering in the long run.

✔ time management training, career coaching, and/or stress counselling are good ways to help recovery and long-term comfort and satisfaction.

Step five: Minimise the outcomes of stress

Exercise, both at work and during your leisure time, is shown to protect against the effects of stress, so look into ways you can incorporate this into your day. For example, you could combine exercise with relaxation techniques via yoga, tai chi, or Pilates. Do check with your doctor before you begin.

Increasing the flexibility you have regarding your tasks at work can also reap rewards. Discuss this with your boss, and explain that having more control over *when* and *how* to achieve your objectives will reduce the impact of work stress on your life.

Increasing your support network can also have a big and positive effect on the way you're feeling: this can range from spending more time with family and friends outside of work to finding a mentor who can bring new insights to the way you live. Maintaining good personal relationships and occupying different roles (such as husband, wife, mum, or dad) are important buffers to stress and will help you to focus on your life outside work.

Good coaching or stress counselling can teach you how to cope better with unavoidable stress. Changing your perceptions or beliefs, modifying your behaviour to gain positive benefits, and negotiating more assertively with others will all help.

Common mistakes

✗ You go into denial

Those most at risk of job burnout are the most likely to deny symptoms such as fatigue and distress, and they are unlikely to seek help or change their behaviour until a crisis dawns. Avoid this by listening to the messages from your body and allowing yourself time to recover from symptoms caused by stress and pressure.

✗ You impose pressure on yourself

If you have a tendency to be over-enthusiastic and ambitious, if you aren't good at asserting yourself, or if you are a perfectionist, it may take some time to change these habits. Try not to expect too much too soon and 'rescue' yourself when you realise you have taken on too much. Pace yourself towards deadlines and map out your time, building in sufficient allowance for the other things in life.

✗ You add to existing stress

Psychologists call this 'problems about problems': under pressure you become concerned about your work, and, as pressure mounts, symptoms of your concern increase until they become more worrying than the initial trouble. For example, let's say you are finding it hard to sleep because of pressure at work. You then start to worry about the effect of the lack of sleep on your performance, so you take sleeping tablets. Now you

Tackling job burnout

worry about the effect of these on your health. As you can see, if you follow this pattern, everything will become increasingly bad, so you need to break the cycle. Concentrate on the root of the problem and take action to balance your demands, supports, and constraints.

✗ You relapse

When you are combating job burnout, give yourself a traffic light system to recognise 'green' comfort zone symptoms, 'amber' stretch zone symptoms, and 'red' stress symptoms. Notice what triggers you to move between these zones and set aside some time regularly to ask yourself 'How do I feel right now? What are the triggers?' Think up some strategies in advance so that you'll know what to do if you feel 'amber' or recognise the onset of 'red' symptoms. The fact of being prepared will, in itself, help you to feel more in control of yourself and your situation.

STEPS TO SUCCESS

✔ Recognise the symptoms of stress—it's an essential step in improving your situation.

✔ Understand the causes and common sources of workplace stress so that you can prevent it becoming an issue.

✔ Take your holiday allowance. You may feel that you cannot be spared, but it's important that you take time

41

off. Your energy and concentration levels will flag without a break.

✔ Talk to your GP about any health concerns you have. Exercise can really help, so try to incorporate it into your work day and leisure time.

✔ Acknowledge that you are burnt out and act upon that knowledge—draw up a plan of action and follow it.

Useful links

Various stress websites:
http://directory.google.com/Top/Society/Work/Job_Burnout
Mindtools.com, 'Life Crises':
www.mindtools.com/smlcu.html
Mindtools.com, 'Avoid Burnout':
http://www.mindtools.com/burnout.html
PsychTests.com, Type A Personality Test:
www.psychtests.com/tests/personality/type_a_r_access.html

Managing dual-career dilemmas

There are many arguments in favour of dual-career families. In most cases, two incomes enable partners to provide at least the basic comforts and modest pleasures of modern life. When both partners work, each is able to keep up with his or her career path, stay marketable and competitive, and contribute to post-retirement financial security. Additionally, the knowledge that one partner is securely employed gives the other partner the opportunity to resign, if necessary, and seek a better position elsewhere.

However, there are also drawbacks: one member of the couple may have to move their career interests down a gear in favour of the other's. Time and energy demands can also distract dual-career couples from their personal priorities: their marriage, their children, and their interests.

Step one: Get your priorities straight

Fortunately, employers are increasingly recognising the need to implement policies that promote flexibility and tolerance for balancing personal needs with work. As an example, many companies are offering flexitime and teleworking, and day-care programmes for children, among other initiatives to help working parents to balance their jobs with their family life. But, as a dual-career couple, you and your partner must still be the ones to make the choices and decisions that best reflect the values and priorities that you've agreed on as a couple.

Only you and your partner can prioritise the elements of your life together according to your values. But the following points are key questions to ask yourselves as you manage your dual career:

- Is each partner's career a primary career?
- How do family needs and career requirements conflict with each other?
- How do family needs and career requirements enhance each other?
- In the case of conflicting opportunities, how will the decisions be made equitably so that, in the long run, both partners will be able to look back with satisfaction?
- How can you make sure the long-term financial interests of the non-primary career partner are protected?

Step two: Agree whether there will be a primary career and a secondary career

If you aren't both going to put your careers first, make sure you both recognise this fact and are happy with this solution. Do be honest—simmering resentment won't help anyone. With this understanding, you know who will be responsible for taking care of a sick child, while the other one attends an important meeting.

If both careers are primary, it's important to understand that as well. Agreeing how your careers fit on the priority list will reduce the potential for major disagreements that could strain your relationship.

Step three: Manage your relationship

It is possible to balance the career that you desire with a healthy relationship—but only if you manage each carefully. Have a clear idea in advance about what you want and agree this with your partner so you can make your choices consistent with your long-term mission. You'll know later whether you achieved that mission.

Work–life balance experts say that you probably won't be able to have this all at once, but, if you work together with your partner, you stand a better chance. How much you truly have all at once depends on your willingness to make trade-offs.

Divorces among dual-career couples may be more common than among single-career couples—but you don't have to sacrifice your marriage for your career. Communication, trust, flexibility, and creativity are important for every partnership and they're especially important for dual-career couples.

If you hit a rough patch, take a businesslike approach to solving the problem. Living a rough and uninspiring life doesn't necessarily mean you're falling out of love—just as a failed product launch doesn't mean necessarily that your organisation is doomed. It could merely mean that you need to alter the management of certain parts of your life.

✔ Approach your dual career as you would a complex business

Understand there are various 'departments' in your private life, and manage them effectively. This isn't to suggest that you shouldn't manage them with love and devotion. But budgeting and compartmentalising certain aspects of your life and time could help you to distribute your resources (time, money, attention) in the most effective way.

✔ Consider your personal partner to be your business partner as well

Just as a company defines long-term objectives and has a mission, work with your partner to determine what your relationship's mission and long-term objectives are. Using long-term missions and objectives as reference points will help the two of you to make difficult decisions when an opportunity for one partner involves great sacrifice for the other.

✔ Communicate

You can only expect your partner to serve your needs and your priorities if he or she knows what they are.

TOP TIP

Make dates and also make appointments with your partner. Appointments are for managing the business of your lives together; dates are for romance!

Step four: Take advantage of technology

Many dual-career homes have at least one computer. Install business-management software that can also automate certain aspects of the business of your life. There are calendar, organisation, and accounting software packages available to give the average consumer the management advantages enjoyed by big business. You can even keep your shopping list on the family computer.

It's not easy to make the transition from depending on a diary and Post-It® notes to organising your life with a computerised device such as a Palm™ Pilot.

✔ Plan the time it will take to learn the new technology and transfer your information. Only allow a month during which you use a dual system; then throw the paper diary away.

New technology can be intimidating, but where there's a will, there's a way. You will soon find your new system as convenient as any other you may have used in the past, if not more so.

TOP TIP
Companies outsource services that are necessary but beyond their internal capability. Why not try this at home if you need to? The services available to you can range from chores such as housekeeping and cooking to support services such as bookkeeping, financial planning, and even marriage counselling.

Step five: Use your business skills training to help you manage your work—life balance

One skill that could serve you well into the future is negotiation. When the two of you take the same course, you'll then negotiate with each other according to the same rules and a shared understanding of ultimate goals.

✔ Recruit your children

There is no reason why dual-career couples with children should shoulder the burden of all the little tasks of living. Give your children age-appropriate responsibilities. Make them partners in your family's future as well as the beneficiaries of your hard work.

Step six: Take care of yourself

You're also the CEO of your own life. Remember to include your own needs in the larger balance of family, work, and partnership obligations. You're no good to anyone if you aren't good to yourself.

Common mistakes

✗ You find that you are 'ships that pass in the night'

It's so easy to get absorbed with the daily details of living and working that you forget to appreciate the life you've built together. Set aside time together that is exclusively for enjoying each other's company. Remember how much you like being together, regardless of what else is going on in your lives.

✗ You lose control of the small details of life

Keeping track of minor details could seem too trivial to prioritise. However, those details could mean the difference between whether or not you have an argument over an empty petrol tank or milk carton — or a forgotten child still waiting to be picked up at an empty school. Keep 'To-do' and 'To Buy' lists at a central location where everyone can keep them up to date. Make sure everyone knows whose responsibility it is to complete those 'To-do' tasks.

✗ You feel as though you're carrying the whole load, both at work and at home

Be sure you continue to communicate with your partner on both daily needs and long-term career goals. If you find that one of you always ends up giving up on personal goals and dreams in favour of the other's, check with your partner to make sure that this trend is acceptable to both of you.

STEPS TO SUCCESS

✔ Prioritise together—understand your values as a couple so that choices and decisions reflect what is most important to both of you.

✔ Understand that not only your career but your relationship must be worked at.

✔ Make firm decisions as to whether one career will be primary, and which, and agree to make allowances for this.

✔ Take advantage of technology and don't be afraid to delegate responsibility—either within the family or with external help.

✔ Make time for yourself, and communicate freely and openly.

Useful links

Anglo Domus, International Relocation Services:
www.anglodomus.com
Net Expat: Dual Career Challenges
www.netexpat.com/dualcareer.htm
Self help tips:
www.kmarshack.com

Reinventing yourself

Sometimes, a complete change of scene is something that seems very attractive. If your career has been in a rut, or if you've been through a turbulent time at home or at work, reinventing yourself may seem to be the key to a fresh start. As a word, 'reinvention' implies a process of deconstruction, followed by reconstruction, and a resultant new thing or—as in this case—a new person who exhibits different talents and who pursues different opportunities. The intended 'payback' for reinvention is gaining something that you currently feel is missing in your life. This could be anything from a successful career to a better financial situation, to a happier work–life balance, or a completely new lifestyle.

Reinventing yourself as a *reaction* to something or to a set of circumstances tends to result in a purely cosmetic change, as it does not get to the root of *why* you want your life to be different. In order to reinvent yourself successfully and for the right reasons, you need to do it consciously and deliberately rather than as a knee-jerk reaction. This doesn't mean for a moment that spontaneity and creativity have no role in a life change—indeed, they're valuable forces in this

process—but building in reality-checks as you go along will do you no harm at all.

Step one: Take stock

Many of us arrive at decision points in our careers unexpectedly. For most people, the planned career path is a myth. It's unusual to find someone who decided what they wanted to do with their careers when they were at school and then followed the recommended route to get there. When people talk about their jobs, it's much more common to hear how amazed they are at what they've ended up doing—listen out for how many times you hear the phrase 'I just seemed to fall into it!'. It's not surprising, then, that many of us eventually realise that we're not doing what rewards us professionally, emotionally, culturally, or spiritually.

The pressures of modern life drive us towards making choices that bring an illusion of security, status, and success. We find a 'good job' and are sucked into the promotional slip stream while being paid an increasingly large salary for taking on additional responsibilities. At the same time, we accumulate benefits such as private health care and company pension schemes which make us reluctant to change our lives radically. Once we realise we're unhappy, we try to rationalise our way out of it, convincing ourselves that we've invested too much in our organisation and our careers so far to risk starting again at the beginning. So we struggle on, perhaps resentfully, fantasising about how it could have been. If only . . .

Sometimes, we're 'fortunate' enough to be assisted in overcoming our resistance to change. We're made redundant, we suffer ill health, our family circumstances change, a significant relationship comes to an end, and so on. This external trigger often results in personal reinvention—and is often perceived to be a blessing in the long run.

The challenge for most people is to arrive at the decision to make adjustments in their lives *before* such a dramatic catalyst intervenes. Being able to sense the imbalance in your life, the drawbacks of your current job, and the gulf between who you are and who you've become is key to making meaningful personal changes. In this way, you can be conscious of what you're doing, why you're doing it, and the likely pay-offs or penalties for doing so.

Below is a process that may help you through the reinvention process:

I Do a personal audit

This is the part of the process where you appraise your life from a personal and professional perspective. You could think of it as a 'force-field analysis', where you write your name in the centre of a clean sheet of paper and itemise your life's pressures and disappointments on the left and the pleasures and delights on the right. Write down everything you think is relevant, including the interests and aspirations that you had early in your career and all the things that have given you happiness since then.

From this activity alone, you may be able to see where unacceptable pressures lie but if you can't, highlight the 'break points' on both sides of the analysis in a highlighter pen so that you can easily identify the issues that really need to be addressed. The intention here is to find a way of swinging the balance of your life towards the pleasurable side of the diagram by drawing out the elements of your life that characterise you and your preferred role.

2 Explore your values and beliefs

If something is preventing you from tapping into your natural talents and living your life in line with them, write it down at the bottom of the sheet of paper. These are the barriers that you have to overcome in order to achieve satisfactory reinvention. They usually manifest as fears, for example: 'I will lose my income/pension/benefits', 'I have a dependent family and can't risk letting them down', 'I have hefty financial commitments and won't be able to meet these if I change my job', or 'I can't afford to go back and start something from the beginning at this stage of my career'.

3 Think about your dream scenario

Think about what you'd do if you were free from practical or financial limitations and write everything down at the top of your sheet of paper. This is a freeing exercise that may put

---

TOP TIP
All these are fears that you hold without
question. So question them. Are they *really*
true? Do they *really* matter? If you live your
life according to these beliefs, how will you
feel at the end of your career? Is this
acceptable to you?

---

you in touch with what it is you would prefer to be doing.
Don't censor your ideas or cast them aside on the basis that
you don't have enough money or security to achieve them—
don't put more barriers in your way and remember that, with
a little imagination and inventiveness, there are ways around
the perceived obstacle of money and security.

Step two: Plan carefully

If you like the company you work for, but aren't sure you
want to remain on your current career path, you have to plan
carefully for your 'reinvention'.

1. First of all, think of a career path within your company
   that you *would* like to pursue.

2. Now work out what your transferable skills and
   attributes are (see chapter 7 for more on this).

3. If you feel there are gaps in your knowledge, think

about how you can fill them, either by training or by gaining some experience on-site. For example, perhaps you could arrange to shadow a colleague who has the experience you're hoping to gain.

4. Once you've done your research and are clear about what you want to do, broach the subject with your line manager or human resources department (if you have one) to discuss how they can support you in making the personal changes you've identified.

It's much better to tackle this situation head-on than to languish in an unrewarding role.

If you worry that your CV reflects who you *were*, rather than who you want to *become*, don't worry—there are bound to be elements in your CV that signpost the direction you'd now like to take, so draw attention to them and explain their relevance to your target job. Also, point out factors in your personal life that mean you're suitable for the role.

Don't be afraid to share your passions and aspirations with your prospective employers—this will help them to see past any omissions in your previous experience. Remember that passion for a role is very attractive to recruiters; just think about how many uninspiring (and uninspired!) applications they have to sift through every day.

Also, remember that you can always rewrite your CV so it is targeted at the job you want to move into.

TOP TIP

If you are concerned about a mismatch between your values and those of your employer, don't ignore your concerns. Values are strong personal beliefs that aren't up for negotiation. You may be able to *appear* to take on values that aren't your own, but, under pressure, your values will reassert themselves.

It's essential that your values match those of your colleagues because otherwise you'll feel continual internal, and possibly external, conflict. Pretending to be someone you're not is too high a price to pay. It's much better to look elsewhere for a new job where your values are shared—it may be a slog, but it'll be worth it in the long run.

Step three: Start making changes

Now you've done the thinking, you can start making changes, small or radical. Working through the process above has allowed you to see your life laid out in front of you and should help you to pinpoint the areas that need the most immediate attention. If you have a strong feeling about the need to change something but aren't clear why, don't try to reason your way out it; follow your instincts and see what happens.

If you curb your impulses by rationalising them, you'll end up behaving in the same way time and time again. To others, and indeed to yourself on some levels, your actions may not stand to reason, but see what happens anyway—many people have benefited from taking risks at certain points in their life. Taking action first and reflecting later has probably been the pattern of your career to date; so try something new, see if it works, and then adopt or discard your initiative as appropriate.

Step four: Live the changes

It's no good deciding to make changes but then not doing anything about it. Even if the changes seem alien to you to begin with, practise them until they feel normal. Act as if you're the best artist in your field, the greatest writer, the most successful entrepreneur—whatever it is you want to achieve. It's mind over matter; once you start behaving like the person you want to be, people will start treating you as if you *are* that person.

Step five: Reinvent yourself

You'll see that reinvention isn't really what's going on here. The *effect* is reinvention; the *fact* is that you're bringing to the surface a latent part of your character that seeks full and happy expression. Make the decision to live the way you want to fully and without apology. What's the worst that can happen?

TOP TIP
You can't change your life without changing your behaviour patterns, and this will feel strange to begin with. If you find this too hard, try starting with symbolic changes, like your clothing or your car. You could even throw away the television! By doing this, you'll create new reactions in others, or you'll find that you're introduced to new people who will help to draw you further into your desired— promotable—self.

Common mistakes

✗ You rush it

Some people decide to make radical changes in their lives and jump into a reinvention of themselves noisily and clumsily. This only leads to disappointment. Although enthusiasm is vital for any attempts at personal change, it needs to be balanced with considered decisions and a deep understanding of yourself. Without these, you'll make changes that don't last and you'll end up feeling disillusioned and de-energised. Work through the process above and ask a trusted friend to help you if you feel you're getting lost along the way—someone else's perceptions and feedback can be very helpful in keeping you on track.

✗ You feel pressurised by others

There are many pressures driving people towards feeling inadequate if they don't do something 'momentous' with their lives. There's no 'rule' for what you should be, however, so don't get pushed into reinventing yourself for the wrong reasons. Always make sure that it's *your* choice that is driving your desire for change and not external pressure or some 'ideal' that you've adopted. Being happy with who you are should be your objective, not change for change's sake.

✗ You pretend to be something you're not

Reinventing yourself isn't just a marketing exercise, although it may help you to market yourself successfully in your chosen professional area. People are quick to pick up on others who they think are just 'putting on' a new personality or way of acting, so be who you really are, for the right reasons.

STEPS TO SUCCESS

✔ Assess your values and beliefs and identify anything that prevents you from fulfilling these.

✔ Know the ideal situation you would like to live in and decide what you will need to change to get you there.

✔ Don't over-rationalise—follow your instincts and take action.

✔ Don't rush the process—if you take your time and think carefully about what you'd like to achieve, you're much less likely to run out of steam if things don't change immediately.

✔ Don't be pushed into radical changes by other people. What works for them may not work for you.

✔ Change only for you and to be the person you really are.

Useful links

Fast Company:
www.fastcompany.com/online/29/reinvent.html
Fiona Harrold:
**www.fionaharrold.com/course_information/
reinvent.html**
iVillage.co.uk:
**www.ivillage.co.uk/relationships/famfri/emotwb/
articles/0,,161285_553896,00.html**
PsychotherapyHELP:
www.nvo.com/psych_help/reinventyourself1

Making yourself promotable

If you have decided that you want to move on up the career ladder, the next step is to make yourself promotable—another aspect of the reinvention process.

Being promotable combines your professional skills with your business sense and ability to build good relationships. This creates the impression of someone who will be valuable to your organisation at increasingly senior levels. Once you become recognised for your specialist expertise and have a track record of success, you're no doubt likely to be seen as a candidate for the succession line.

As well as your track record, however, the 'powers that be' will also take into account other personal attributes that go well beyond your current role. To get ahead, you'll need to demonstrate business acumen, political sensitivity, the ability to manage change, and loyalty to your employing organisation. These attributes go hand-in-hand with the need to communicate and network effectively and the ability to cement critical relationships with those who will sponsor and support you as you move along your career path.

Step one: Ensure that you are considered

When competition is fierce, it is important to do everything you can to make sure that you are considered to be a suitable candidate for a new appointment. However, blowing your own trumpet too loudly isn't always the most effective way of influencing events. Being clear about what you want and why you deserve to be promoted is, of course, very important, but a subtle approach can also reap rewards. You could, for example:

✔ find a mentor or sponsor in the organisation with whom you can work

✔ approach your line manager and discuss your development plan in the light of your conviction that you have more to offer the business

✔ observe those who have been promoted and ask yourself if you're projecting the same personal attributes

In some organisations, promotion is a thing of the past for all but a very few people—usually in the senior management tiers. These are:

■ **flat organisations:** there are fewer levels in the hierarchy

TOP TIP
Try to become more visible by ensuring that
you take the opportunity to mix with decision-
makers and by sharing stories of your success
at appropriate times. Don't make too much of
your achievements or you may turn off the
very people you need to court.

■ **matrix organisations:** the business is structured
according to common activities rather than discrete
business units. Project teams are made up of
specialists from across a business.

In such organisations, promotability takes on a new meaning,
as there is often no clear succession route. There may be
prestigious and exciting areas to be associated with,
however, or some career-enhancing assignments that you
could target. Take a step back and examine the patterns and
trends of progressive career paths in your organisation.
Once you've identified the 'hot spots', you can work out
which suit you best and plan your approach to reach them.

Step one: Build a winning personal 'brand'

Making yourself promotable is not an easy task because it
implies a very wide development agenda. Aspects of this
include:

✔ familiarising yourself with the broader business arena and general management issues.

✔ developing social and political skills that enable you to build effective relationships.

✔ finding a personal leadership style that you're comfortable with and that can develop into a distinctive personal 'brand' in the long run.

It's a sad fact that the personal skills and attributes that have carried you to the point in your career where you're looking at a more senior appointment are the very skills and attributes that can sabotage your success at this level. These include having too high a dependence on your specialist expertise, an individualistic approach that differentiates you from your peers, and an inclination to challenge the organisational status quo. Shedding some of these traits, therefore, may be the key to becoming promotable.

Step two: Develop good interpersonal skills

As you progress through your career, a shift occurs in the balance between the expert contribution you make and your ability to build relationships. More senior roles demand a higher level of political sensitivity because at this level relationships go beyond the organisational setting and are more likely have an impact on the long-term viability of the business. Faced with this realisation, many potential leaders try to fake it with an over-confident communication style that conveys nothing but arrogance and authoritarianism.

Good interpersonal relationships are built by people who have no axe to grind and who aren't trying to create an illusion of confidence and capability. There's no substitute for genuine self-confidence; people can generally see through bluff and blag, so it's important to put the time in to really know yourself well, understand your values, and create a clear picture of what you want.

Step three: Meet business objectives

In order to make yourself promotable, not only do you have to meet the objectives of your role, but you also have to contribute to the wider business. This means showing initiative and taking an interest in areas outside your role boundaries. You could do this by volunteering for an important project, chairing a committee, or facilitating a special interest group. If you're seen to be supportive of, and passionate about, the business, you're much more likely to be noticed as someone who could add value at a more senior level.

Although it may be unpalatable to some, you could consider (subtle) ways in which you can broadcast your willingness to play a more committed part in the fortunes of your business, such as suggesting or volunteering for a special project. This doesn't mean that you have to be sycophantic, but if you act like someone who occupies the type of role you're aiming for, it'll be easy for others to see you in that role.

TOP TIP
While increasing your 'visibility' within the boundaries of your organisation is important, you don't need to confine yourself to just that. Why not publish articles in your trade or professional magazine, or accept invitations (or volunteer) to speak at conferences? If you want to raise your visibility more locally to demonstrate your commitment to your community, you could get involved in local politics.

Step four: Build and lead teams

One of the essential skills of a senior executive is the ability to build and lead teams. Without this the co-operative networks—which are vital to an organisation if it is to achieve its objectives—are damaged. Much of a person's success in this area depends on his or her ability to communicate clear objectives as well as understanding the skills, motivations, and personal values of those in their team. Relationships must be open, with a healthy ebb and flow of feedback to ensure that everyone is aligned with the purpose of the team. Milestones and markers need to be part of the plan so that progress can be monitored and successes celebrated.

Step five: Learn to manage transition and change

Business and organisational models change in response to developments in the market and economy. The ripple-effects of these changes are felt throughout the organisation and have an impact on everyone. Being able to field such changes and use your knowledge and insight to direct people's creative energy towards making them a success are valuable attributes of a leader. Showing reluctance and other blocking behaviours are not perceived to be helpful, even if you feel that the change is unwise or counter-productive.

If you find yourself in a situation like this, you may want to make alternative suggestions and explain the thinking behind them. If your concerns are rejected, though, demonstrate your loyalty by remaining flexible and actively seeking ways of making the changes work. Show that you're prepared to keep people motivated and learn from the new experience rather than being resentful or obstinate.

TOP TIP
Remaining flexible, actively seeking ways of making (sometimes difficult) things happen, keeping people motivated, and learning from the new experience are all important characteristics of those in the top team. Loyalty and solidarity are values that are prized in cultures that are subject to transition and change.

Step six: Build an effective network of champions or sponsors

We've all seen people who have been promoted on the basis of who they know, not what they know, yet this is no guarantee of future success. Indeed, investing in a nepotistic relationship is all very well when your champion is in favour, but, if their reputation is damaged for any reason, yours will also be tarnished because of your close association.

It's important, therefore, to build a robust network of relationships with people who will support you purely because of your potential and personal integrity. In this way, you can be sure that you aren't reliant on the perception people have of someone else (and over whom you have no control), but that you're judged on your own talent and attributes.

Think about your network and identify role models, potential coaches, and mentors for different aspects of your development plan. As you approach them, be open with your request for assistance but beware of projecting self-interest above the interests of the organisation. Frame your request in development terms, stating that you feel you have more to offer the business and would appreciate their guidance.

In summary, being promotable does not rely on past success but on your ambassadorial qualities as you represent those in the upper echelons of the organisation. Neither does it rely on over-confidence or bullishness. Being promotable demands that you demonstrate:

- an active interest in the business and an understanding of the strategic issues
- an ability to reach targets and build value
- a genuinely confident communication style
- an ability to build effective personal relationships within your team and amongst your colleagues

Common mistakes

✗ You irritate the people who could help you

Sometimes, people looking for a move up the career ladder damage their case by making so much noise around the people who they think can promote them that their efforts become irritating and counter-productive.

There are unwritten 'rules' to being promotable, and you need to work these out by observing and adopting some of the tactics of successful people who've gone before you.

✗ You're not willing to change

Although a track record of being a maverick may get you noticed, this is usually not a trait that will get you promoted. You need to play down your notoriety and redirect your energies into activities that are seen to support the organisation's best interests. If you're hoping to enter a different cultural zone in the organisation, you have to make sure you're familiar with the values that operate there and demonstrate that they're part of your value set too.

✗ You ignore your team

It's tempting to focus on yourself as you look towards your career horizon and plan for your own success. You'll be judged on your ability to develop the talent in your team, though, so it's foolish to ignore them. You won't succeed by squashing those with potential, so you must trust in your own abilities and let your team flourish too. Doing this will create a loyal group who will support you in the long run. Take care to maintain these relationships as you move through the organisation, as you never know who you'll be working with (or for!) one day.

STEPS TO SUCCESS

✔ Find alternative ways to make yourself noticed without being boastful.

✔ Familiarise yourself with the skills and approach necessary to succeed in your workplace and work hard at developing these.

✔ Build good personal relationships and be aware of others' needs.

✔ Expand your capabilities outside your specific role—take an interested and active part in the wider business of your company.

✔ Refine your leadership skills and learn to be flexible and accommodating of change.

✔ Work with those around you to support your cause—this means not only building up a contact network but being careful not to offend existing and potential colleagues.

✔ Don't ignore your team. Do all you can to help them develop effectively—this is another powerful way of establishing yourself in your workplace.

Useful links

Dauten.com:

www.dauten.com/promotable.htm

iVillage.co.uk:

www.ivillage.co.uk/workcareer/survive/archive/

0,,156470,00.html

OCJobSite.com:

www.ocjobsite.com/job-articles/promote-yourself.asp

Knowing when it's time to move on

Very few people stay in one job or at one company or one organisation for their whole career these days. Deciding to leave a familiar job and familiar faces can be hard, though, and there's a lot to think about. The best time to go is when you feel your role will no longer meet your objectives beyond the short-term, or when you feel there are other roles out there that will bring you closer to the future that you want.

Common reasons for moving on are:

- your role turns out to be different from the one advertised
- your role isn't interesting
- there are no further opportunities for you within the business
- no development activities are planned
- you're not given enough support
- you disagree with the organisation's values or ethics
- you're treated badly by your boss or colleagues
- stress levels are too high
- grievances are not dealt with professionally
- the grass is greener elsewhere

Recognising the right point to leave a job is difficult. The trick is to be clear about what's important to you; once your priorities and goals are established, the decision becomes much clearer.

Step one: Be sure of what you feel

Take a moment to acknowledge your feelings, as decision-making is an emotional as well as a rational process. What are the main issues and how do you feel about them? Write down words that describe your reactions to the important issues facing you. When you have finished, review what you have written and try to understand what has prompted these emotions. This is important work for two reasons:

■ If you decide to stay in your current job, you need to come to terms with these reactions and find strategies for coping better in the future.
■ If you decide to move on, you'll need to address and 'park' these issues and emotions for good in order to start afresh, leaving old insecurities and problems behind.

TOP TIP
Be sure that leaving is the right thing for you before you go ahead and do it. For financial reasons, most people wait until they have found another job before they hand in their

**notice, but sticking it out when work's a
nightmare may be the wrong thing, as your
confidence is sapped and your health suffers.
Leaving in order to job hunt is quite a risk and
isn't possible for everyone, but, if you can do
it, it will give you more time to find the right
next role and will free your mind to focus on
the future.**

Step two: Do a reality check

Think about what you really want from a role, keeping it
realistic and bearing your long-term career plan in mind.
This will give you a list of the criteria against which you will
weigh up your current role and any offers you get in the
future.

Start with a blank sheet of paper and divide it in four. What
are the elements of your ideal job? For example:

- What kind of **organisation** do you want to work for?
  Some factors you may consider are size, sector,
  environment, philosophy, attitude to staff, prospects for
  learning, and opportunities for promotion.
- What are the ingredients of the ideal **role**? What would
  be your main focus, type of activity, travel, status (full- or
  part-time), and hours?
- What do you want in a **boss**? Someone hands-on or
  hands-off? A mentor with a consultative style or
  someone who can give a prescriptive lead?

■ What will make up your ideal **package**? What would be your basic pay, bonus, car, and holiday allowance? Factor in what you'd want in terms of relocation package (if appropriate), flexible working options, and overtime.

As an example, here's a fully-worked reality check for someone who works in HR.

Ideal organisation	**Ideal role**
Has a charismatic leader with a vision that works in reality	Working in a team, able to spark off each others' ideas
Communicates a clear strategy	Friendly team at work (possibly socialise outside work)
Actually implements, rather than pays lip-service to, that strategy	Variety and novelty
Tangible products/services or output	Stimulating work with plenty of challenges
Meaningful products or services that I can be proud of	Opportunities for progression
Not a status-driven organisation	Some elements familiar or drawing on processes I already know
HR represented on the board	Using my current HR expertise
Respect for employees	Good communication between parts of the business.
Nice offices	
Efficiently run	

Ideal boss	Ideal package
Knowledgeable	£40K salary plus:
Provides clear direction, then hands-off	Pension scheme
Supportive, able to mentor	Medical insurance and life policy
Manages the boardroom relationships well	Car and parking or season ticket
Imposes deadlines	5 weeks' holiday
Direct but caring	Family-friendly policies
Empathetic, sensitive	Flexitime, so I'm not tied to 9–5 every day
Appreciative	
Great motivator	

Step three: Look at what you've got

Now take another sheet of paper and divide it in the same way. You've just identified the criteria you're looking for in an ideal role, so now you need to rate your *current* role on each of the criteria on a scale of 1–10, where 10 is ideal and 1 is totally unbearable. Write comments for each rating too, such as what it would take to make things better, the extent to which you are in control of the situation, and how likely it is that things may change in the near future.

Now review this plan. You may just have one or two criteria with terrible scores and recognise that, if you can find a way to improve these, it may be worthwhile staying. Perhaps you can use your reality check to talk through the issue with your boss? If you're going to do this, remember to balance the discussion about what you want or need from a role with positive comments on what you are giving and your employer is getting in return.

If, on the other hand, you see several areas where your current role is just not working for you, it's probably time to cut your losses and find an alternative.

Step four: Check out your options

It's time to review the market. Until you are clear about what you might be moving on to, it's impossible to weigh up the decision properly.

Start with a list of the options and go through each one, asking yourself: 'What do I need to know about this to decide if it's for me?' Then decide how you will get that information: you could try the Internet, a contact, a professional body, or another way. As you research the options, some will start to look more and more interesting, while others may have barriers or sticking points. As you research, the list usually gets shorter, as some options prove to be impracticable, but you may discover more options as you go—it all depends on you, what you want, and what's available at any given time.

You may want to concentrate on options in your local area. Put out some feelers by scanning newspapers, calling two or three recruitment agencies, and visiting local companies' websites. Finally, think about the timing. You may decide to change job when the market is at its most competitive or you may decide to stick to your current job until the market picks up and your chances of getting the role you want increase.

How to find out what other roles are out there

The Internet is a fantastic resource for research of this type, and there are many job-related sites online. These allow you to target your search by industry, job title, salary, and location.

Simply talking to other people can also be an effective way of exploring the job market, though. People are very good at making associations based on partial information—that is, they can see links or patterns that you might not have noticed, and may have come across occupations that you've never even heard of. Strike up conversations with friends, family, ex-colleagues, and ex-bosses—anyone you can think of, really—and tell them you are considering the future and wondering what other options there are for you. Briefly explain your main skills and strengths and ask them what jobs they can imagine you doing well. The information you get may be interesting, stimulating, and surprising—but try not to get too carried away with it until you have followed it up with some research of your own.

Step five: Make the decision

Analyse the pros and cons using your BRAINS:

- **Benefits:** in what way would you benefit from staying where you are?
- **Risks:** what would you risk if you stayed?
- **Advantages:** what are the advantages of moving on?
- **Implications:** what are the implications of moving on?
- **Now:** is now the best time for this move?
- **So . . . what do I feel about this decision?**

Common mistakes

✗ You jump from the frying pan into the fire

So you hate your job and have been offered something that looks better. Should you accept it? Accepting the first role that is offered in order to get away from an unbearable situation may seem fine at first, but if you rush the decision it too can turn out to be a nightmare. Go carefully through a reality check and politely request enough time to get the information you need. Don't rely on the 'hype' of either the job advert or your prospective employer. Ask the new organisation if you can talk to some members of the department you'll be joining to satisfy yourself that it is the right decision for you before you sign on the dotted line.

✗ You lack the confidence to negotiate

If you are keen to get a new job, it's easy to feel that you should just take what is offered, but ask yourself:

- Will I be happy with this package in 6 months' time?
- Is this pay above or below the average for the market?
- Is this pay similar to or different from my future colleagues'?
- Would I still be happy if I had to work a lot of overtime?

There may also be elements other than the package that you've identified from your reality check as not quite right for you. To tackle these, wait until you get the written contract, identify what the issues are, and then call your future employer to ask what can be done to improve these elements. Remember to make it clear how interested you are in the role so that your prospective new bosses don't feel as if they've been given an ultimatum. Remind them of what you'll be bringing in terms of skills and strengths and of the ways in which the role fits your profile, then allow them time to come back to you with an adjusted offer.

STEPS TO SUCCESS

✔ Decision-making can be emotional as well as rational. Take the time to acknowledge your feelings so that you can deal with them whatever your final choice.

✔ Be certain that you want to move on by weighing what you have in your current position against what you would want in an ideal role. If you're unhappy about just one area of your working life, you may be able to sort it out.

✔ If you do decide to move on, do plenty of research before you leap. To make the right decision you must be clear about what you will be moving on to.

✔ Be sure about what you are looking for. Have an ideal role, boss, and benefits package in mind, as well as the type of organisation you'd like to work for.

✔ Use your BRAINS to finalise the decision.

✔ Don't be too hasty; be prepared to negotiate to get your perfect job.

Useful links

BBC One Life—Work Index:
www.bbc.co.uk/radio1/onelife/work/index.shtml
Friends Reunited Jobs:
www.friendsreunitedjobs.com
Totaljobs.com:
www.totaljobs.com
Job Search:
www.jobsearch.co.uk

Where to find more help

How to Get a Job You'll Love: A Practical Guide to Unlocking Your Talents and Finding Your True Career
John Lees
McGraw-Hill Education, 2004
250pp ISBN 0077108248
Using skills he has learnt in his own career as a career transition coach and career strategist, Lees presents a refreshing look at career planning. To overcome mental barriers that might prevent you from changing career, a simple five point plan is suggested. The book also includes tips on job search strategies and how to succeed in interviews.

Choosing Your Career: Work Out What You Really Want To Do With Your Life
Sally Longson
Kogan Page, 2004
160pp ISBN 0749441038
Aimed at those feeling anxious about making decisions in the first stages of their career, this book offers self-assessment exercises and practical tasks to help readers decide on the best career path. The guide helps readers to identify their personal strengths, desires, and opportunities.

The Penguin Careers Guide
Jan Widmer
Penguin Books Ltd, 2004
736pp ISBN 0141013761
The newest edition of a long-standing and highly respected title, *The Penguin Careers Guide* is an invaluable resource for those seeking career information. Details of over 300 careers are included, with notes on the required qualifications, the nature of

the work, desirable personal attributes, and training, as well as advice for late starters and those returning to work.

Career Change Handbook: How to Find Out What You're Good at and Enjoy – and Get Someone to Pay You for It
Graham Green
How To Books, 2004
208pp ISBN 1857039580
This is a book written to inspire the reader to bring about a change in their working life. Written to help readers to find out more about themselves in relation to the world of work, this book explains the philosophy behind career change, while offering step-by-step guidance through the job search process.

Make It Happen: How to Get Ahead and Be Happy at Work
Dena Michelli, ed
A & C Black/Bloomsbury, 2005
288pp ISBN 0–7475–7237–2
We spend over 70% of our week at work, so being happy while we're there is a major priority. This book sets out to help readers make the most of their talents and build the career they want. Edited by Dena Michelli, author of the best-selling *Assertiveness in a Week* (Hodder), the book offers practical advice on more than 60 common career challenges so that you can go to work with confidence; achieve your full potential; and manage successful teams.

Get Yourself Promoted: How to Move Up the Career Ladder
Steps to Success series
A & C Black, 2006
96pp, ISBN 0–7136–7519–5
Being good at what you do isn't enough to help you clamber up the career ladder these days – you need to make yourself 'promotable'. This means having a magic mix of great skills and personal qualities that enable you to meet your targets, build good relationships with other people, and get to know the people you can help you during your campaign. Covering everything from planning your career to

finding out about 'hidden' job vacancies and making yourself indispensable, this book offers advice and useful hints on how to get your foot on the next rung of the career ladder.

I Don't Know What I Want, But I Know It's Not This: A Step-by-step Guide to Finding Gratifying Work

Julie Jansen
London: Piatkus, 2004
270pp ISBN: 0273675826

A useful resource for anyone unhappy at work. Full of exercises to assess the reader's personality and skills, this book will help people to understand their present situation and come up with ways to find the job or career they really want to embark on.